Kitten Trouble

Written by Inbali Iserles

Illustrated by Max Rambaldi

Collins

I am Bob and I'm living my best life.
I love my family.

Mummy Mim keeps my bowl full of yummy food.

Mummy Becky loves to take me to the park.

Look, a rainbow!

Foz's cuddles are the best.

4

I am springy. I am happy.
Until someone new joins the family ...

One day, Mummy Mim comes home with a kitten.

The little kitten has her own toy mouse. But she chews my best teddy instead.

The little kitten gets cuddles from Mummy Mim.
She gets snuggles from Mummy Becky.

Suddenly, the house is full of relatives who have all come to see the kitten.

The kitten gets tickles and cuddles all the time.

No one plays with me. It's not fair!

I am gloomy. I am grumpy. I am feeling sorry for myself.

Jelly is my enemy.

It is a frosty night. Mummy Mim, Mummy Becky and Foz are all asleep.

There is a bright starry sky through the window.

I am too sleepy to play with Jelly.

Go away, Jelly.

Suddenly, I hear a creepy sound from the next flat. Somebody is there with a torch.

It's a thief! I start barking angrily.

Mummy Mim hears the noise. She calls the emergency number.

There is a thief in the next house!

Jelly and I have saved the day! Everybody praises us. Next day, Mummy Becky cooks a fancy meal to celebrate.

I suppose Jelly did help a little bit.

She's funny.

Bob and Jelly

❀ **Review: After reading** ❀

Use your assessment from hearing the children read to choose any GPCs, words or tricky words that need additional practice.

Read 1: Decoding

- Turn to page 5 and point to the word **springy**. Ask the children to read the sentence and explain what a "springy Bob" is like. (e.g. *jumping around with happiness, excitable*)
- Encourage the children to read multi-syllable words, breaking them down into chunks if necessary.

fam/il/y	**in/stead**	**some/bod/y**
spring/y	**rel/a/tives**	**em/er/genc/y**

- Ask the children to take turns to read a sentence aloud. Encourage them to sound out the words in their heads silently. Say: Can you blend in your head when you read the words?

Read 2: Prosody

- Turn to pages 10 to 13, and discuss who the narrator (Bob) might be getting a bit jealous and fed up with by now.
- Model making the sentences convey how grumpy Bob is feeling. Emphasise **full** in the sentence on page 10.
- Challenge the children to use intonation and expression to sound grumpy when Bob is speaking on pages 13 and 16.

Read 3: Comprehension

- Talk about the title, and ask the children what sort of things they have seen or read about kittens that might make them troublesome.
- Reread pages 20 and 21, and ask: Do you think Bob's feelings about Jelly changed by the end of the story? Why?
  - Turn to page 18, and discuss the experience Bob and Jelly shared. (*seeing a thief and making a noise*)
  - Ask the children to imagine other events that might make Bob like Jelly (e.g. *they play hide and seek*) or be cross with Jelly (e.g. *he has to have a bath but the kitten doesn't*).
  - Encourage the children to develop an event into a story. Ask: What happens before and afterwards?
- Look together at pages 22 and 23. Challenge the children to use the pictures to help them retell the story in sequence.